More!
Instant
Bible
Lessons
for Preschoolers

I Have Fun at Church

Pamela J. Kuhn

These pages may be copied.
Permission is granted to the buyer of this book to
photocopy student materials in this book for
use with Sunday school or Bible teaching classes.

Rainbow Publishers

Rainbow Publishers • P.O. Box 261129 • San Diego, CA 92196
www.rainbowpublishers.com

To Brianna Lynne:
Though I have not seen you yet (still so tiny and so far away!) I love to look at your picture.
It makes me feel so warm when I see your sweet smile. I know Mommy and Daddy will teach you
to read all about Jesus. With love, Auntie Pam

MORE! INSTANT BIBLE LESSONS FOR PRESCHOOLERS: I HAVE FUN AT CHURCH
©2010 by Rainbow Publishers, first printing
ISBN 10: 1-58411-072-4
ISBN 13: 978-1-58411-072-9
Rainbow reorder# RB36858
RELIGION / Christian Ministry / Children

Rainbow Publishers
P.O. Box 261129
San Diego, CA 92196
www.rainbowpublishers.com

Interior Illustrator: Hallie Gillett
Cover Illustrator: Tammie Lyon

SUSTAINABLE FORESTRY INITIATIVE

Certified Chain of Custody
Promoting Sustainable
Forest Management
www.sfiprogram.org

Scriptures are from the *Holy Bible: New International Version* (North American Edition), ©1973, 1978, 1984 by the
International Bible Society. Used by permission of Zondervan Bible Publishers.

Printed in the United States of America

Contents

Introduction

Wecome to *I Have Fun at Church*, a book packed full with useful lesson activities for your preschoolers. You'll find the lively Bible stories and kid-friendly activities make it easy to teach essentials about children's participation in church, such as singing, praying, worshiping, and inviting friends. Engage your students with active games and songs, set to familiar melodies, along with age-appropriate puzzles and worksheets. You'll find clear directions and lists of materials for the crafts and snacks, so you'll always be ready to go.

Each of the first eight chapters includes a Bible story, memory verse and numerous activities to help reinforce the lessons about the ways you have fun at church. An additional chapter contains projects that can be used anytime throughout the study or at the end to review the lessons. Teacher aids, including bulletin board ideas and discussion starters, are sprinkled throughout the book.

The most exciting aspect of the *More! Instant Bible Lessons for Preschoolers* series is its flexibility. You can easily adapt these lessons to a Sunday School hour, a children's church service, a Wednesday night Bible study, a Christian school classroom or family home use. And, because there is a variety of reproducible ideas from which to choose, you will enjoy creating a class session that is best for your group — whether large or small, beginning or advanced, active or studious.

This book is written to add enjoyment to learning about the ways we have fun at church. Teaching children is exciting and rewarding, especially when you successfully share God's Word and its principles with your students. *More! Instant Bible Lessons for Preschoolers* will help you accomplish that goal. Blessings on you as your students explore how they have fun at church.

How to Use This Book

Each chapter begins with a Bible story for you to read to your class, followed by discussion questions. Then, use any or all of the activities in the chapter to help drive home the message of that lesson. Each activity is tagged with one of the icons below, so you can quickly flip through the chapter and select the projects you need. Simply cut off the teacher instructions on the pages and duplicate as desired.

craft   finger play   teacher help   bulletin board   activity

puzzle   action song   song   game   snack

Chapter 1
I Have Fun at Worship

Memory Verse

True worshipers will worship the Father.
John 4:23

Story to Share
King Josiah Repairs the Temple

Josiah was only 8 years old when he was made king. When King Josiah was 16, he began to worship God. No king loved God more than Josiah did.

Josiah had noticed that many of his people had begun to worship idols. But Josiah wanted his whole kingdom to worship God. For six years, Josiah worked to get rid of the idols. He had the altars used to worship idols torn down, and the idols ground into dust.

Because so many people were worshiping idols, God's temple was not cared for properly. When King Solomon had built the temple, he had richly decorated the building to honor God. The walls and floors had been lined with carved cedar wood and gold. Even the doors and door posts had been beautifully carved. But it had been 250 years since repairs were made to the special temple.

Josiah was only 26 years old, but he knew it was important to have a place to worship God. He gave orders for the temple to be repaired.

Money was collected to buy the materials needed for the repairs. The men chosen to work on the temple were honest and could be trusted to work hard. They bought wood and stone to make repairs. When the temple was repaired, Josiah brought back the singers and musicians to celebrate.

God was pleased with the young king. He wants His house to be clean and in good repair. Josiah led the people in making a new vow of love and loyalty to the true God of Israel.

— Based on 2 Kings 22:1-6

Discussion Questions

1. How old was King Josiah when he gave orders for the temple to be cleaned? (26)
2. Are you old enough to help keep the church clean? (yes)

Scroll Holder

snack

What You Need
- duplicated page
- card stock
- crayons
- fruit leather
- straws
- glue

What to Do
1. Duplicate scroll holders to card stock and cut out one for each child.
2. Allow the children to color their holders.
3. Help the children fold and glue their holders.
4. Give each child a fruit leather and two straws. Show how to roll the ends of the leather onto the straws.

What to Say
The scroll represents the Bible. Remember to bring your Bible to church each Sunday. One of the ways we can worship God is to learn about Him. Our Bible tells us how God wants us to live. (As you tell the story each week, open your Bible to show the story is from God's Word.)

Worship

God's Word

is for Me!

We Worship God

We go to church
to worship God,
Worship God,
worship God.
We go to church
to worship God,
Every Sunday
morning!

Continued from right...

the green grass along the bottoms of the white papers. Go around and staple the ends. Cover the staples with tape to avoid injury.

7. Instruct each child to glue the children pattern to a craft stick.

8. Show how to slip the end of the craft stick through the bottom slit between the white paper and grass. "Walk" the children to church while singing "We Worship God" to the tune of "This Is the Way We Wash Our Clothes."

craft

· · · · · · · · · · · · ·

What You Need
- duplicated page
- white and green construction paper
- crayons
- glue
- stapler
- tape
- craft sticks

What to Do
1. Duplicate the children and church for each child.
2. Pre-cut white construction paper in half. Cut green construction paper into 8½" x 2" strips. Cut a fringe in the green construction paper to make the strips look like grass.
3. Allow the children to color their churches and children.
4. Instruct the children to glue their churches on the left sides of their white papers.
5. Allow the children to draw yellow suns in their skies.
6. Show how to lay

Continued at left...

Worship

9

Path Sewing Card

craft

What You Need
- duplicated page
- card stock
- crayons
- yarn
- tape
- hold punch

What to Do
1. Duplicate sewing card patterns to card stock. Cut out one card for each child.
2. Punch a hole in the child and in every footprint.
3. Cut yarn in 20" lengths. Wrap tape around one end of each yarn length to make it stiff. Tie a knot at the opposite end of each one.
4. Allow the children to color their sewing cards.
5. Show how to lace the yarn through the hole by the child on the card and tape the knot to the back of the card.
6. Demonstrate how to "sew" the card to get the child to church.
7. Do this activity as a class, repeating the word of each footprint until you arrive at the church.

Worship

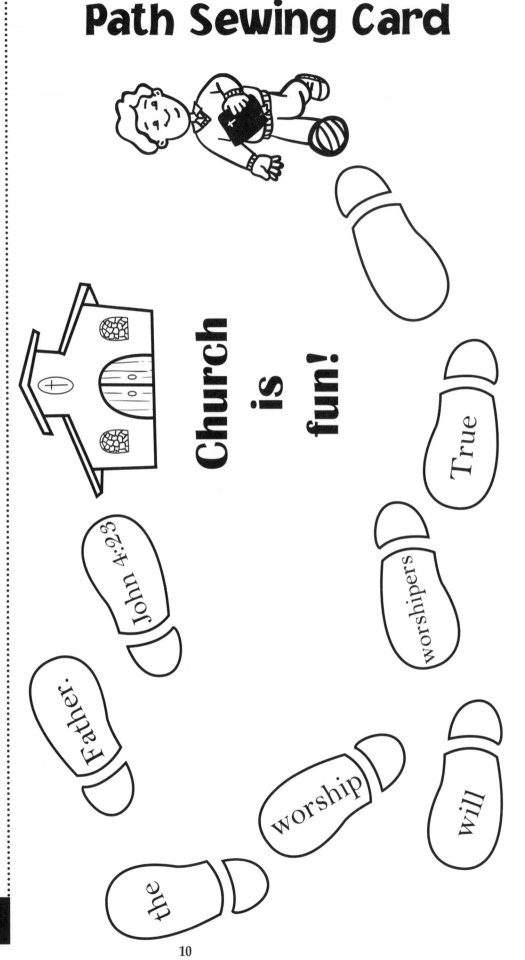

Church is fun!

True

worshipers

will

worship

the

Father.

John 4:23

King's Treat

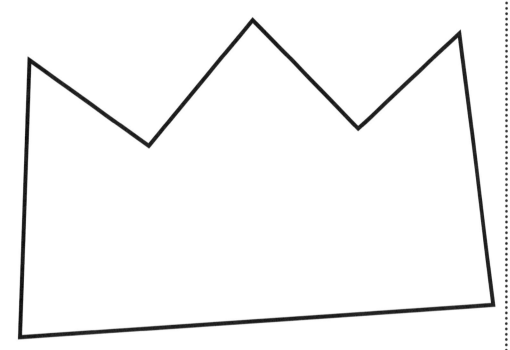

What You Need
- duplicated page
- bread
- butter
- sugar
- cinnamon
- sprinkle container
- gem-shaped fruit snacks

What to Do
1. Using the crown pattern, cut a crown from bread for each child. Mix sugar and cinnamon in a sprinkle container. Spread the bread crowns with butter.
2. Give a crown to each child, allowing him or her to sprinkle the crown with the cinnamon/sugar mixture.
3. Give the children fruit gems to decorate their crowns.

What To Say

In Bible days there were good kings and evil kings. What made the good kings different? (They loved God) How are we different when we love God? (We are obedient, loving, helpful, kind) One way we can show God we love Him is by coming to worship Him at church.

Worship

finger play

What You Need
• duplicated page
• pencils/crayons

What to Do
1. Duplicate a worksheet for each child.
2. Instruct the children to circle or color the items that can be used to keep the church clean.
3. Say the finger play with the children.

Clean Church Worksheet

I may be very little, (point to self)
And my muscles kinda small. (flex muscles)
But I can use my hands and feet,
(hold out hands and point to feet)
To keep my church clean and neat.
(fold hands with pointer fingers forming steeple)

Church Bus Fun

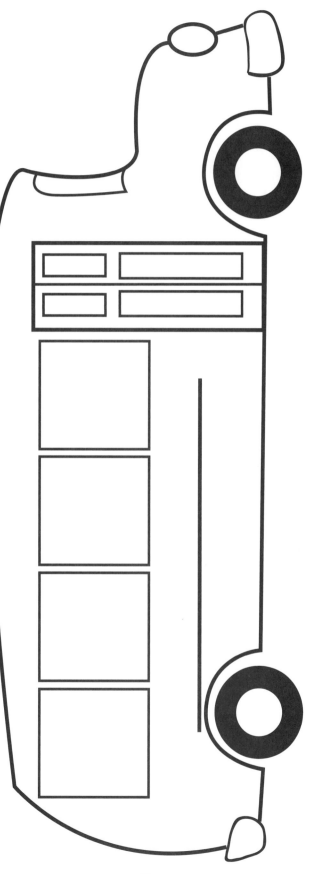

Comin' to church and bringin' my Bible.
Comin' to church and bringin' my Bible.
Coming to church and bringin' my Bible.
So I can worship God!

craft

What You Need
- duplicated page
- card stock
- glue
- crayons

What to Do
1. Print the name of your church on the side of the bus.
2. Duplicate buses to card stock and cut out one for each child. Also duplicate and cut out a set of children for each child.
3. Allow the children to color their buses and pictures. Instruct the children to glue a child picture to every bus window.
4. Allow the children to "drive" their buses as you sing the song to the tune of "Picking Up Pawpaws."
5. You can draw a church on the chalkboard, then have the children line up with their buses at the opposite wall and allow them to "drive to church."

Worship

craft

What You Need
- duplicated page
- crayons
- glue
- construction paper

What to Do
1. Duplicate and cut out a set of church pieces for each child.
2. Allow the children to color their church pieces.
3. Show how to glue the pieces to the construction paper to form a church.
4. Instruct the children to draw a scene (sun, birds, trees, flowers, etc.) around the church.

What to Say
The people in Bible times called their place of worship a temple. What do we call our place of worship? (a church)

Continued on next page...

Worship

Build a Church

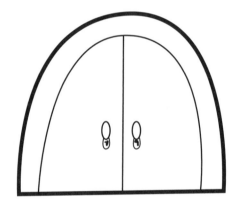

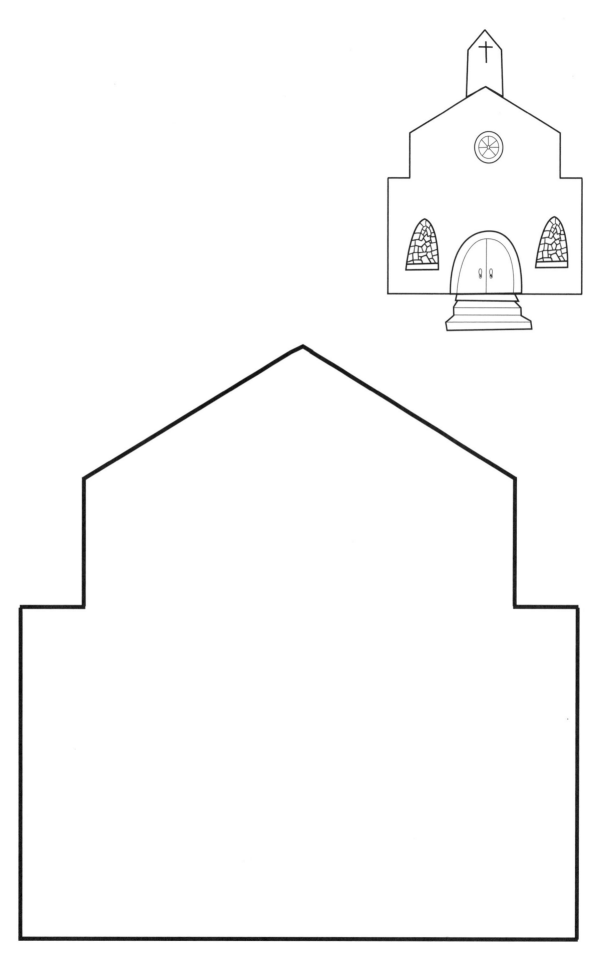

15

craft

What You Need

- duplicated page
- dessert-size paper plates
- crayons
- paper fasteners

What to Do

1. Duplicate and cut out a church for each child.
2. Cut the rim off a paper plate for each child.
3. Before class, use a craft knife to cut out the dashed window in each church.
4. Allow the children to color the churches.
5. Help each child attach his or her church to a paper plate with a paper fastener.
6. Go around and write each child's name in his or her church window, turning the wheel and adding every child's name in the class. Let those who can print add their own names.

Attendance Spinning Wheel

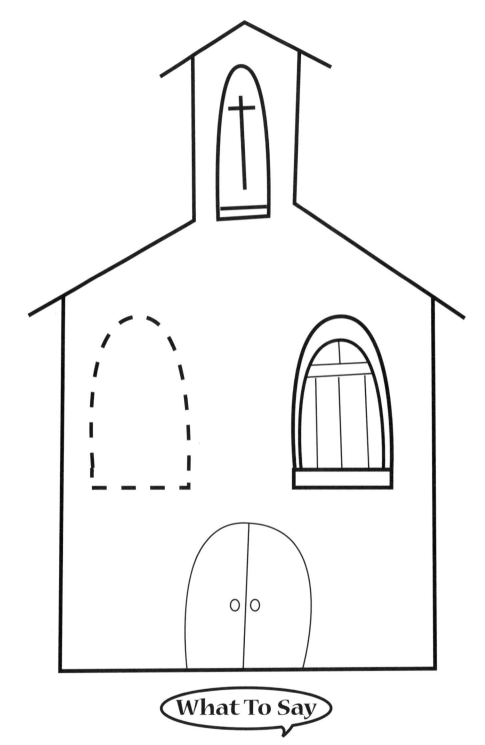

What To Say

Why are we in church today? (to worship God) Let's turn our wheels and say, "(Kayla), I'm happy you are here today!"

Chapter 2
I Have Fun Giving at Church

📖 Memory Verse

A generous man will prosper.
Proverbs 11:25

📖 Story to Share
A Woman Gives All

When Jesus was in Jerusalem, He loved to spend time at the temple. One day while Jesus was there He saw many people coming to the temple, bringing their offerings with them. The temple offering box hung on the wall. The top of the box was hinged and could be opened when someone wanted to give an offering.

As Jesus watched, He saw many wealthy men empty full money bags into the box. Many of the wealthy men wanted others to notice how much they were giving to God. They would wait until someone was nearby, then they would empty their bags with a flourish, making sure the coins clanged together to draw even more attention to their gifts.

Then Jesus saw a woman walking toward the box. She was a lonely widow woman who missed her husband. In Bible days, widows had very little money to buy food and clothes. Jesus saw that she carried a bit of cloth in her hands. When the woman reached the offering box, she opened the cloth she was holding. There were two small copper coins in the cloth. She placed them in the box, barely lifting her head to look around. She knew it was a small offering, but it was all she had.

Jesus' eyes were full of tears as He looked at His disciples.

"This woman's offering amounts to more than all of the offerings received today," He said.

The disciples didn't understand what Jesus meant. They had seen the two small coins, too. And they had seen the many gold coins put in by wealthy men.

"The wealthy men gave only a small portion of what they have," said Jesus. "They won't even miss the amount they gave. This woman gave God everything she had."

— Based on Luke 21:1-4

❓ Discussion Questions

1. Do we need to give to God even if we don't have much to give?
2. What can you give to God?

craft

What You Need

- duplicated page
- craft foam sheets
- craft foam shapes
- glue
- chenille stems
- coins
- offering plate
- hold punch

What to Do

1. Trace the coin purse pattern on foam. You will need two for each child.
2. Punch holes around the purses.
3. Thread a chenille stem through the first hole in each pair of front and back pieces, bending and twisting to attach the pieces.
4. Show the children how to "sew" their purses with the chenille stem.
5. Allow the children to choose a foam shape to glue to the front of the purse.
6. Give each child a few coins to put in his or her purse. Have a march offering, singing the song to the tune of "The Farmer in the Dell."

Giving

March Offering

What will you give to God?
What will you give to God?
When we give, we worship Him.
What will you give to God?
I'll give my coins to God.
I'll give my coins to God.
When I give, I worship Him.
I'll give my coins to God.

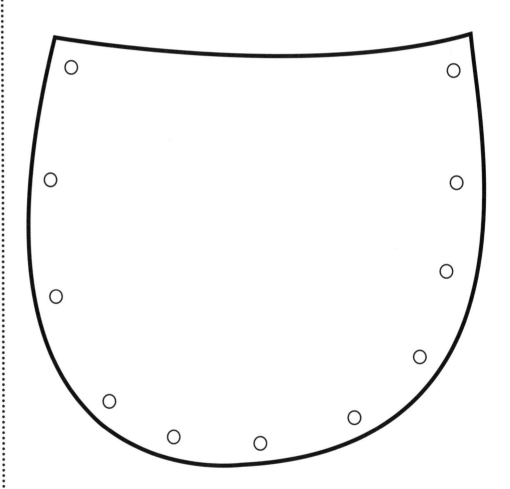

Give Your All

craft

What You Need
- duplicate page
- crayons
- hole punch
- paper fasteners
- tape

What to Do
1. Duplicate and cut out a set of pictures for each child.
2. Allow the children to color the pictures.
3. Assist the children in punching small holes where indicated and threading paper fasteners through to fasten book pages. Cover the ends of the fasteners with tape to prevent injury.

What to Say
There are many ways that giving to God helps us worship. Giving our money is one way. Other ways are giving our time to invite others to church, giving our smiles to cheer others and giving a hug to warm our pastor's heart.

Giving

puzzle

What You Need
• duplicated page
• crayons

What to Do
1. Duplicate a worksheet for each child.
2. Show how to look at each row of coins and decide which two are play money and should not go into the offering plate.
3. Instruct the children to draw a line from each real coin to the offering plate.

What to Say
Why does God want us to give money in the offering?

Coins for the Offering Plate

Giving

20

Penny Poem and Verse Review

craft

What You Need
- duplicated page
- crayons
- safety scissors
- offering basket

What to Do
1. Duplicate a penny for each child.
2. Allow the children to color and cut out their pennies.
3. Say the verse and choose a child to put his or her penny in the basket. As the child puts the penny in, instruct him or her to say the verse. Many of the children might need help with the verse – say it with them until they know it.

What to Say
We don't have to have a lot of money to give to Jesus. He can see our generous hearts.

There was a little woman,
With a coin tight in her hand.
She gave it all to Jesus,
It was the best offering in the land.

A generous man
will prosper.
Proverbs 11:25

Giving

21

Penny Wrap

snack

What You Need
- duplicated page
- pita bread
- peanut butter
- bananas
- plastic knives
- crayons
- safety scissors
- glue
- clear, self-stick plastic
- 6" foam plates
- wet wipes

What to Do

1. Before class, cut pita bread into pie-shaped pieces. Cut bananas into round pieces. Cut clear plastic into 4" circles, one per child.
2. Allow the children to color and cut out the coins.
3. Instruct each child to glue the coins to a foam plate.
4. Go around and cover each child's coins with a clear plastic circle.
5. Give each child some peanut butter and banana slices along with a knife.
6. Allow the children

Continued at right...

Giving

Continued from left...

to spread peanut butter on the pita pie shapes. Show how to begin at the large end and wrap the pita around the banana slice.

7. Say a thank-you prayer for the food.
8. After the snack, wipe the plates and allow the students to take them home.

The Widow's Penny Coloring Picture

activity

What You Need
- duplicated page
- crayons
- pennies or toy coins
- glue

What to Do
1. Duplicate a coloring picture for each child.
2. Allow the children to color their pictures.
3. Give each child two pennies to glue to the widow's hand.

What to Say
See the patches on the woman's shawl and robe? The woman could have saved her coins to buy some new clothes. Instead, she gave her money to church. Save some coins for Jesus instead of buying a candy bar, soda or book.

Giving

Jumpin' Pennies

game

What You Need
- duplicated page
- clear, self-stick plastic

What to Do
1. Duplicate six pennies on brown paper.
2. Write a word from the memory verse on five pennies and the scripture reference on the sixth penny.
3. Cover the pennies with clear plastic and cut them out.
4. Lay the pennies on the floor, jumping distance apart.
5. Allow the children to jump from penny to penny as you say the words to the verse.
6. Use this activity when you have a few extra minutes of class time. Not only will it help to get rid of some wiggles, it will reinforce the verse in the minds.

Giving

Puzzle Piece Fun

puzzle

What You Need
- duplicated page
- crayons
- paper sacks
- envelope

What to Do
1. Duplicate and cut out a puzzle piece set for each child.
2. Allow the children to color the pieces. Go around and write each child's name on the back of his or her pieces.
3. Place all of the pieces in a bag.
4. Pass the bag, instructing the children to take a puzzle piece out of it. Continue the bag around the circle; the children will take a puzzle piece out each time it passes. If the child draws a piece twice, he or she should pass the repeated piece to a friend. See who can complete the puzzles first!
5. Give each child an envelope to take his or her puzzle home.

Giving

Chapter 3
I Have Fun Inviting Others to Church

Memory Verse

You are the light of the world.
Matthew 5:14

Story to Share
Come and See

The disciples and those who loved Jesus were sad. They had watched as Jesus' body was put in a tomb. Afterward, Jesus' friends went home to cry.

Three days later on Sunday morning, Jesus' mother and some other women walked to the tomb where Jesus was buried. They brought spices to put in the tomb so it would smell good. Imagine their surprise when they found it empty! Not only did they find an empty tomb, they found an angel there to greet them.

The women started at the shining angel.

"He is not here, He is alive!" the angel said, pointing to the grave clothes in the tomb.

"Go," the angel said. "Go and tell Jesus' disciples that He has risen."

For a moment, the women could only stare at the angel. Then they turned and began walking back toward town. Faster and faster they walked until they gathered up their skirts and ran. The expensive spices they carried fell to the ground as they ran.

Seeing Peter, the women stopped. At first he couldn't understand what they were trying to tell him. They were so excited that they spoke all at once!

"Stop, slow down," Peter said. "Just one of you speak."

Mary Magdalene clutched at his arm. "It's Jesus," she said. "He's not dead. He's not in the grave. He's alive!

Peter stared at her. "What?" he asked in astonishment.

"It's true," Mary said with a joyful laugh. "Come and see!"

— Based on John 20:1-18

Discussion Questions

1. What exciting news did Mary tell Peter about Jesus? (He's alive!)
2. What exciting news can you tell your friends about Jesus? (He loves them, He will forgive their sins)

snack

What You Need
- duplicated page
- tall baby food jars
- crayons
- glue
- milk
- instant pudding
- plastic spoons

What to Do
1. Duplicate a jar wrap for each child.
2. Allow the children to color their wraps and glue them around their jars.
3. Pour milk into the jars so they are three-quarters full. Add 2 teaspoons of pudding mix to each one.
4. Assist each child in tightly twisting on the cap.
5. Instruct the children to shake their jars. When the mixtures thicken, give each child a spoon to enjoy the surprise.

Inviting

Surprise Snack

You are the light of the world. Matthew 5:14

You are the light of the world. Matthew 5:14

When your friends want to know what you do in church, you can say, "We hear stories, sing songs, play games and make a craft." Then you can tell them, "Snack time is always a surprise, but it's always something yummy."

Tomb Wiggle Buster

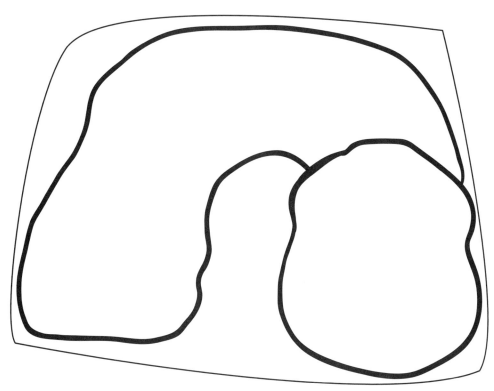

game

What You Need
- duplicated page
- crayons
- masking tape

What to Do
1. Duplicate the tomb, angel and Mary.
2. Lay the pictures and crayons on a table for early arrivals to color.
3. Make a long line on the floor using masking tape. Make another line 2 feet from the first, another 2 feet from the second and another 2 feet from the third. You will have made 3 sections. Place the tomb on the wall or floor in the first section, the angel in the second and Mary in the third.
4. Instruct the children to stand facing the first section. When you say, "Jesus died," the children should jump to the tomb. When you say, "He's not

Continued on next page...

Inviting

29

game

Continued from previous page...

here," the children should jump to the angel. When you say, "Come and see," the children should jump to Mary.

5. Mix up the commands and see how well the students do. End the game with "Come and see."

What to Say

We didn't live when Jesus was on earth and died. We didn't get to see the angel that announced He had risen from the dead. But we can go and tell others it happened. We can invite them to come and worship.

Inviting

Story Sequence
Worksheet

puzzle

What You Need
• duplicated page
• construction paper
• crayons
• stapler
• tape
• glue

What to Do
1. Duplicate a worksheet for each child.
2. Discuss the pictures, allowing the children to point out the first picture in the story sequence. Draw a number one on the board and instruct the children to print "1" in the correct box. Continue with the other pictures.
3. Allow the children to color the pictures.
4. Staple construction paper together to make books. (Cover the staples with tape to prevent injury.) Help the children cut the pictures apart and glue them in the books. Allow time for the children to "read" their books.

Inviting

31

Shining Your Light

puzzle

What You Need
- duplicated page
- crayons

What to Do
1. Duplicate a worksheet for each child.
2. Discuss each picture. Ask, "Does it look like the boy [or girl] is shining for Jesus?"
3. Instruct the children to draw "Xs" on those who are not letting their lights shine.
4. Allow the children to color the pictures of the children who are letting their lights shine.

What to Say
When you are mean to others, they don't know you belong to Jesus. But when we are kind and caring, they know you are different—you have Jesus in your heart!

Light Pencil Topper

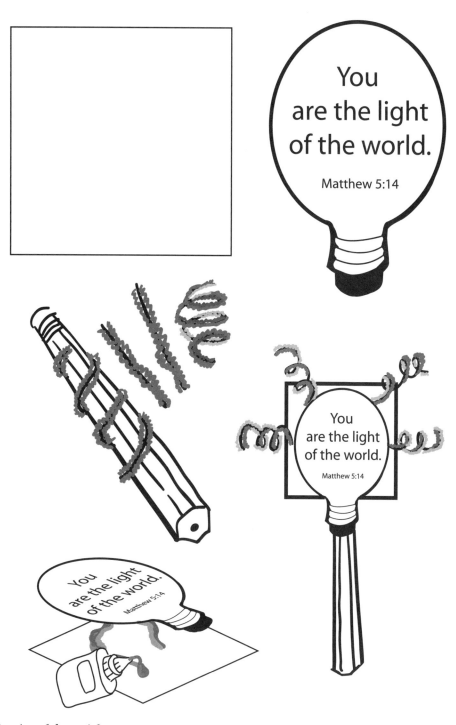

You
are the light
of the world.

Matthew 5:14

craft

What You Need
- duplicated page
- chenille stems
- crayons
- glue
- unsharpened pencils
- aluminum foil
- clothespins

What to Do
1. Duplicate and cut out a light bulb and square for each child.
2. Give each child a light bulb and allow him or her to color it.
3. Cut chenille stems in half. Give each child four halves and an unsharpened pencil. Instruct the children to wrap one end of each stem around the end of a pencil to curl it.
4. Give each child a small piece of foil to wrap around the bottom of the light bulb.
5. Assist the children in gluing the light bulb to the square,

Continued at left...

Continued from right...
leaving the middle unglued for the pencil top and sandwiching the chenille stems between the bulb and square. Clip clothespins to the pieces until they are dry.

What to Say
When someone tells you how cool your pencil looks, say "Thank you," and invite him or her to church.

Inviting

33

puzzle

What You Need
• duplicated page
• crayons
• safety scissors
• glue

What to Do
1. Duplicate a worksheet for each child.
2. Allow the children to color and cut out the pictures.
3. Read the statement under the first dashed square. Allow the children to find the correct picture and glue it in the square. Continue with the other two squares.

What to Say
We should treat the friends we invite to church with respect. These are good ways treat all our friends in our class.

Inviting

Guest Etiquette

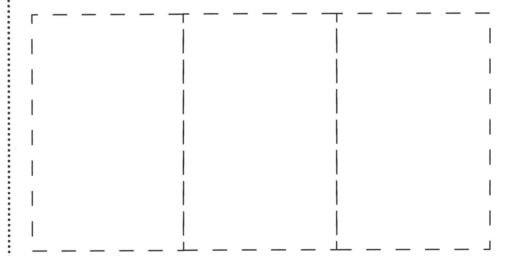

Welcome the guest to your class

Share art supplies with the guest

Allow the guest to go ahead of you in line

You are the light of the world. Matthew 5:14

Air Freshener Invitation

What You Need
- duplicated page
- yarn
- glue
- crayons
- spray cologne
- hole punch

What to Do
1. Duplicate an invitation for each child.
2. Allow the children to color their invitations.
3. Instruct the children to fold their invitations on the dashed lines and glue the backs together.
4. Assist each child in punching holes where indicated on the invitation and tying a piece of yarn through for a hanger.
5. Spray the invitations with cologne.

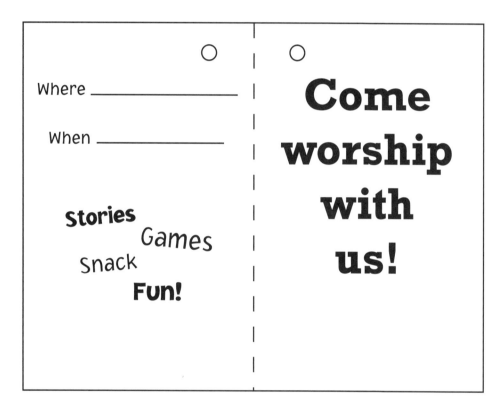

Where _____

When _____

Stories
Games
Snack
Fun!

Come worship with us!

What To Say

Do you like to come and worship God? It makes God happy when we worship Him. He's happy, too, when we bring our friends to worship Him. Hang your air fresheners in your rooms. The scent will remind you to invite friends to attend church with you.

Inviting

35

Felt Board Invitation

song

What You Need
- duplicated page
- poster board
- felt
- crayons
- glue

What to Do
1. Duplicate and cut out a set of pictures and a song sheet for each child.
2. Cut poster board into 5"x 7" pieces, one for each child. Glue felt to one side of each one. Glue a song sheet to the back of each one.
3. Allow the children to color the pictures.
4. Cut felt into 2" squares. Instruct the children to glue each of their pictures on a felt square.
5. Demonstrate how to put the pictures on the board.
6. Have the class sing the song to the tune of "The B-I-B-L-E" as they play with the boards.

C-H-U-R-C-H
Please come to church with me!
It's fun to learn how to worship God,
C-H-U-R-C-H!

The B-I-B-L-E,
Come and learn with me.
We'll hide God's Word down
deep in our heart,
The B-I-B-L-E!

It's J-E-S-U-S,
Come and learn with me.
We'll learn to worship God's own Son,
It's J-E-S-U-S!

Inviting

Memory Verse

Lord…teach me your laws.
Psalm 119:108

Story to Share
God Gives Us Rules

While the Israelites were camping at Mt. Sinai, God gave them 10 special laws to help them know how to live and worship Him better. God gave these rules to Moses to share with His people. These laws are recorded in the Bible. God still wants us to follow them today.

Four of the rules were about God. We should worship God only – the one true God. We shouldn't bow down to idols, or love anything or anyone more than we love God. God doesn't want us to make fun of His name or say it in anger. God wants us to spend one day every week in rest and worship. God said, "Remember the Sabbath day, and keep it holy."

Then God told Moses to teach the people to honor their parents. He does not want us to disobey or disrespect our parents.

"Don't take the lives of others," God then said. "And if you are married, keep your wedding vows."

God also gave us the laws that say "Don't take what isn't yours" and "Don't lie or deceive anyone." The tenth law God gave was "Don't wish you could have something that belongs to someone else. Be happy with your own belongings."

God gave us 10 rules to live by. These are 10 rules we can learn to help us worship God better.

— Based on Exodus 20

Discussion Questions

1. How many rules did God give Moses to help us worship and live right? (Ten)
2. How can we learn God's laws? (listening in church, asking our mommy or daddy to read from the Bible)

puzzle

What You Need
• duplicated page
• crayons

What to Do
1. Duplicate a worksheet for each child.
2. Show the children how to draw a line between the paths to connect the things that go together.

What to Say
Buildings and people looked different in Bible days. Even their Bible looked different from ours today. One thing remains the same – we must learn about God.

What Goes Together?

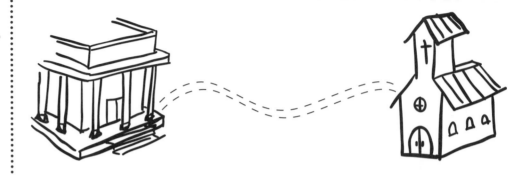

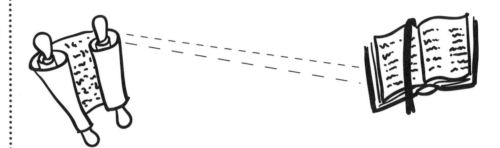

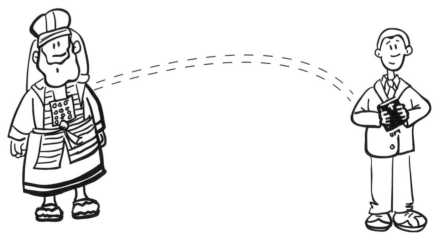

Learning

Learning Is Fun!

snack

What You Need

- duplicated page
- banana slices
- blue gelatin powder
- paper plates

What to Do

1. Duplicate, color and cut out a set of pictures.
2. Give each child banana slices and some gelatin powder on a plate.

What to Say

Today we're going to learn something fun! Dip your yellow bananas into the blue gelatin powder. Does anyone know the powder's new color? (green) We just learned that when you mix something yellow with something blue you get something green. Jesus wants us to learn when we worship God, too. (Hold up pictures) You can learn that God created the earth, that Jesus died for our sins, and that Jesus loves everyone.

Learning

I Can Learn About God

What You Need
- duplicated page
- crayons

What to Do
1. Duplicate a worksheet for each child.
2. Discuss the pictures. Ask, "Who is teaching us about God in this picture?"
3. Allow the children to color the pictures.
4. Read aloud the sentence at the bottom of the page. Instruct the children to trace the letters then say the sentence together.

Learning

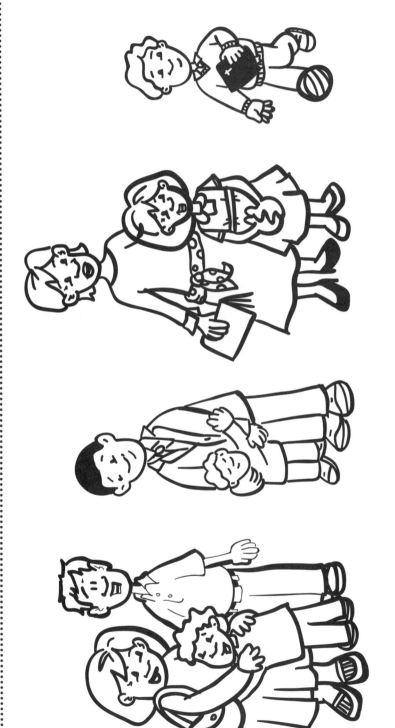

I can learn about God.

Lord...teach me your laws. Psalm 199:108

Grow with God

Grow, grow, grow
with God.
Grow with God
each day.
We must learn
to fear the Lord,
Growing in His way.

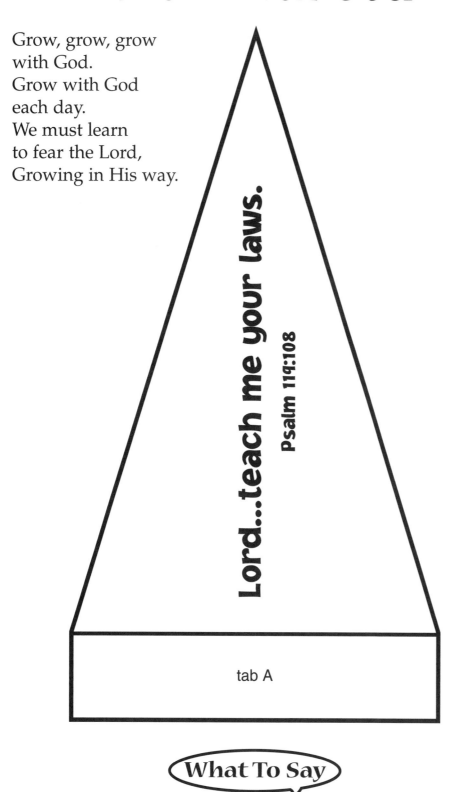

Lord...teach me your laws.

Psalm 119:108

tab A

What To Say

Our memory verse says we should "fear" God. That doesn't mean we should be afraid of Him. It means we should respect and honor Him. One way we can learn to honor the Lord is by learning to obey Him, and parents and teachers. If you learn to obey quickly now, you'll remember to obey when you grow big and tall, too!

song
. . . .

What You Need
- duplicated page
- crayons
- plastic drinking straws
- floral tape
- silk flowers

What to Do
1. Duplicate and cut out a pennant for each child.
2. Allow the children to color their pennants.
3. Assist each child in holding the silk flower stem along the side of a straw and twisting the floral tape around both pieces.
4. Instruct each child to glue the pennant around the top of the straw, gluing the back of Tab A to the back of the pennant.
5. Allow the children to hold their pennants and squat down. Instruct them to "grow" as you sing the song to the tune of "Row, Row, Row Your Boat."

Learning

puzzle

What You Need
- duplicated page
- safety scissors
- glue

What to Do
1. Duplicate a worksheet for each child.
2. Allow the children to cut out the sentence shapes.
3. Instruct the children to glue the shapes to their matching dashed-line shapes.
4. Read the sentences in the shapes. Ask the children which shape's sentence is not a law God gave Moses.

What to Say
God wanted Moses and the Israelites to learn about Him. When you learn God's law to honor your father and mother, you will obey when they tell you to feed the dog. When you learn God doesn't want you to steal, you won't take a toy that doesn't belong to you. Learning about God helps you do what is right.

Learning

Cut, Match, and Paste

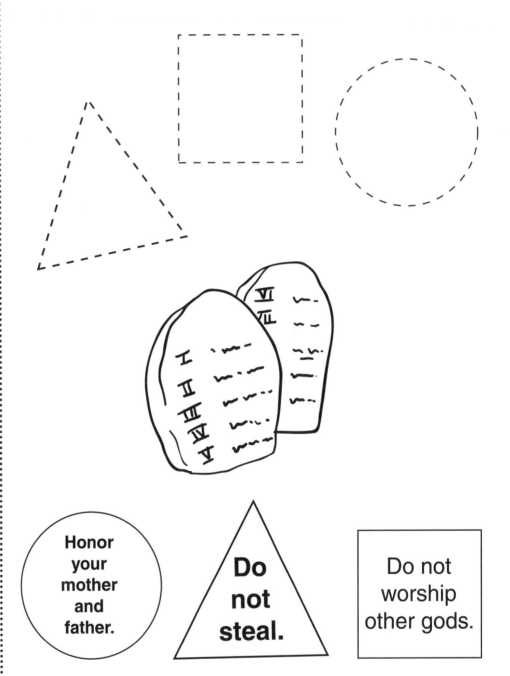

Honor your mother and father.

Do not steal.

Do not worship other gods.

Don't forget to feed the dog.

A Standing Bible Reminder

What You Need
- duplicated page
- card stock
- crayons
- safety scissors
- glue
- cross sticker

What to Do
1. Duplicate two Bibles for each child to card stock.
2. Allow the children to color and cut out the Bibles.
3. Instruct the children to snip the dashed lines.
4. Show how to slip the two Bibles together through the slits to make the Bibles stand upright.
5. Encourage the children to repeat the memory verse. Assist those who need help. Give each child a cross sticker to put on his or her Bible.

Lord... your

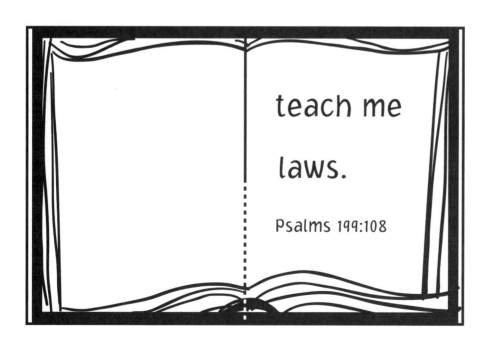

teach me laws.

Psalms 199:108

Learning

A Ten Commandment Sequence Game

game
What You Need
• duplicated page
• crayons
• safety scissors

What to Do
1. Duplicate a worksheet for each child.
2. Allow the children to color and cut out the pictures.
3. Ask the children to put the Bibles in order from small to large. Then ask them to put the Bibles in this order: small, medium, large, small, medium, large. Then ask them to remove the medium-sized Bibles and put the rest of the Bibles in the following order: small, large, small, large.
4. Assist the children in putting the pictures in order if they have difficulty with the activity.

Moses decided to learn and obey the laws of God – all 10 commandments. You can make the same decision, even though you are young.

Learning

44

That's True/That's Not!

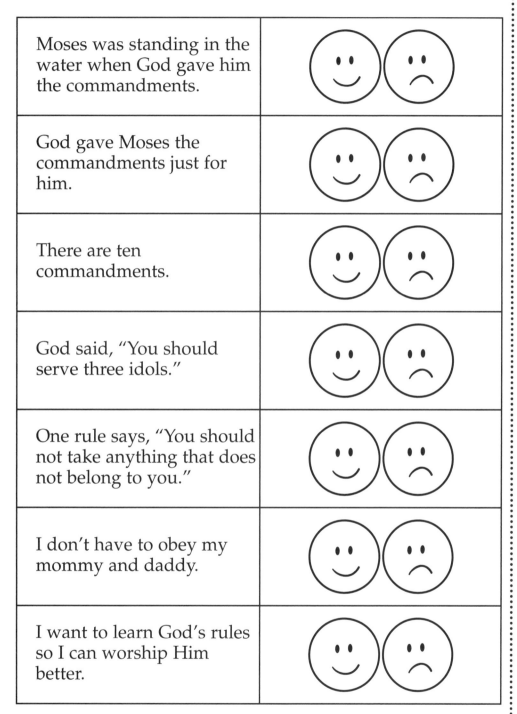

Moses was standing in the water when God gave him the commandments.	😊 ☹️
God gave Moses the commandments just for him.	😊 ☹️
There are ten commandments.	😊 ☹️
God said, "You should serve three idols."	😊 ☹️
One rule says, "You should not take anything that does not belong to you."	😊 ☹️
I don't have to obey my mommy and daddy.	😊 ☹️
I want to learn God's rules so I can worship Him better.	😊 ☹️

Answers:
1. False: he was on Mount Sinai.
2. False: they are for everyone.
3. True.
4. False: serve only Him.
5. True.
6. False: honor your father and mother.
7. True.

What You Need
- duplicated page
- crayons

What to Do
1. Duplicate a worksheet for each child.
2. Read the first sentence aloud. Allow the children to decide whether the statement is true or false. If false, encourage the students to make the statement true.
3. Instruct the children to circle the smiley face for true and the frown for false.

What to Say
The words from the Ten Commandments are in our Bible today. God wants us to learn and obey His Bible too.

Learning

Chapter 5
I Have Fun Praising God at Church

Memory Verse

Praise...him...in the house of the Lord.
Psalm 135:1-2

Story to Share
Praise in the Temple

Jesus was traveling from Jericho to Jerusalem. Wherever He went, a crowd followed. This particular day, two blind men were along the road Jesus was traveling. They could hear someone special was about to pass by them.

"Who's coming?" they asked a nearby man.

"It's Jesus!" he replied.

As soon as the blind men heard that the Son of God was coming, they began shouting.

"Have mercy on us, oh, Lord!" they called as He passed.

Those around them tried to shush them, but Jesus heard.

"What do you want Me to do for you?" He said as he stopped to face them.

"We want to be able to see," the blind men said.

Jesus reached out and touched their eyes. Immediately, they could see Jesus. They looked around to see the crowds. They saw the trees and the blue sky. Then the men joined the crowd following Jesus.

The crowd continued to grow as Jesus rode His donkey into Jerusalem. The people were happy to see Jesus. When Jesus arrived at Jerusalem, He went to the temple to worship. The crowds followed and joined those in the temple who wanted to hear Jesus teach. They also wanted to see Jesus work miracles. The children began singing about Jesus.

"Hosanna!" they sang in their best praise voices. "Honanna to the Son of God."

Jesus smiled when he heard their songs.

"Listen to the children sing," He told the disciples. "The Bible teaches us that small children sing their praises to God more sweetly than anyone else. Everyone should praise God."

— Based on Matthew 20:29-21:17

Discussion Questions

1. How were the children worshipping God in the temple? (by praising Him)

2. What are some ways we can worship God with our praise? (with prayers, songs)

The Praise Game

game

What You Need
- duplicated page
- yellow paper
- smile/frown face
- basket
- yarn

What to Do

1. Duplicate a praise game set to yellow paper and cut it out. Put the cards in a basket. Duplicate and cut out a face pattern.

2. Fold the smile/frown face on the dashed line. Cut an 8" length of yarn. Fold the yarn in the middle. Glue the face backs together, catching 1" of the yarn ends. Hang the faces by the loop.

3. Allow a child to pick a card out of the basket. Read the card to the child and ask if the sentence sounds like someone is praising God or grumbling. Let the child turn the face to a frown or smile to correspond with the card.

I'm too tired to get up for church.	It's Sunday! We get to go to church!
I don't like to color.	Why do I have to wait for my turn?
Thank you for teaching me about Jesus.	I don't want to sit by her!
I love our Pastor.	Bible stories are boring.
I'm glad Jesus loves me.	I'll tell you why I love Jesus.

What To Say

We are going to play a praise game. What does your face look like when you praise God? (happy—make happy face) What does your face look like when you grumble? (frowny—make frowny face)

Praising

48

Puppy Praise

What You Need
- duplicated page
- crayons
- glue
- paper fasteners
- black and brown felt
- hole punch

What to Do
1. Duplicate and cut out a puppy and tail for each child.
2. Using the puppy's spots for a pattern, cut spots out of felt.
3. Let the children color their puppies.
4. Give the children felt spots to glue to their puppies.
5. Attach a tail to each puppy. Show how to help the puppy wag its tail.

What to Say
What do kitties do when you make them happy? (purr) What do puppies do when you feed, pet or play with them? (wag their tails) What can we do to show God we are happy He made us and gives us good things? (sing and wave our arms in praise to Him)

Praising

craft

What You Need
- duplicated page
- crayons
- paper plates
- hole punch
- ribbons

What to Do
1. Duplicate the verse words and church for each child.
2. Give each child a paper plate and instruct him or her to fold the plate in half, right sides together.
3. Allow each child to glue the verse words to one side and the church to the other.
4. To create the handle, cut through both thicknesses of the paper plate, making a 1"x 3" rectangle in the plate, one inch from the fold. (Do not allow the children to do this step.)
5. Allow each child to use a hole punch to make five holes through both sides

Continued at right...

Streamers of Praise

Praise...him... in the house of the Lord.

Psalm 135:1-2

Continued from left...
of their paper plates.
6. Give each child five 12" lengths of ribbon to thread through the holes. Assist in tying the ribbons as close to the paper plates as possible.
7. Sing praise choruses while the children move their streamers in a figure eight pattern.

What to Say
God loves colors – He's the one who created all the colors. God will be happy when He sees us sending our colorful praises to Him.

Praise Notes

Praise...him...
in the house
of the Lord.

Psalm 135:1-2

activity

What You Need
- duplicated page
- bingo daubers
- crayons

What to Do
1. Duplicate a praise picture for each child.
2. Give each child a chance to use the bingo dauber to fill in the praise notes. As the child presses the dauber on a note, instruct him or her to share with the class one thing for which he or she is thankful.
3. Allow the children to color the rest of their pictures.
4. To help a child choose the thing for which he or she praises God, ask questions like, "What is your favorite food?" or "What did God create for us that helps us run?"

Praising

snack

What You Need

- popcorn popper
- large sheet
- popcorn

What to Do

1. Lay out a large sheet on the floor. Allow the children to sit on the edge of the sheet.
2. Sing the song to the tune of "It's Bubbling" while the popcorn pops. Instruct the children not to touch the popcorn until it has cooled.

What to Say

"Popcorn," "poppin" and "praise" all begin with the same letter. They go together, too, because popcorn pops and our praises should pop, too. Can we think of some things that start with the letter "P" for which we can praise God? (people, pets, pilots, pineapple, pine trees, picnics, etc.)

Poppin' Praise Snack

I'm poppin',
I'm poppin',
I'm poppin' up with praise.
I'm poppin',
I'm poppin',
I'm poppin' up with praise.
Praise for God in heaven,
Who's giv'n so much for me.
I'm poppin', poppin', poppin', poppin',
Poppin' up with praise!

Praising

52

One of a Kind Praise

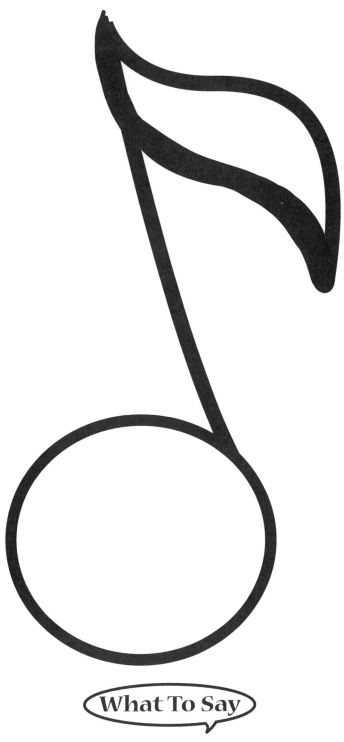

craft

What You Need
- duplicated page
- watercolor paints or crayons
- lettering

What to Do
1. Duplicate a music note for each child.
2. Print each child's name on the stem of a note.
3. Allow the children to decorate their music notes.
4. When the notes are finished, hold up each one and discuss the patterns.
5. Post the notes on a bulletin board with lettering that says "We're One of a Kind!" Write the memory verse along the bottom of the board.

What To Say

All of the notes you painted are beautiful. But they are all different, too. We know God likes things different because He didn't make any of us exactly the same. You might have red hair and green eyes or brown hair and blue eyes. We can all praise God differently, too. Some sing their praises; others praise God in their prayers. You even might want to dance and wave your arms when you praise God.

Praising

53

finger play

What You Need
- duplicated page
- crayons
- tape

What to Do
1. Duplicate five finger puppets for each child.
2. Allow the children to color their puppets.
3. Assist each child in taping the ends together and putting his or her puppets on one hand.
4. Say the finger play. Call on each child to jump up and share one thing for which he or she is thankful.
5. Instruct the children to take off one puppet for each verse. Continue playing until every child has had a turn.

Praising

Five Little Kids

Five little kids
sitting in the church,
Five little kids,
like birds on a perch.
Up jumped [Katie]
With something to say.
"I praise God for [ducks]."
Then she went on her way.

(Repeat with four little children,
three, two and one.)

Now the church is empty,
No praises can be heard.
But they'll be back again,
Singing praises like a bird!

Banner of Praise

craft

What You Need
- duplicated page
- purple felt, 24"x12"
- gold felt
- felt squares, various colors
- glue
- gold ribbon
- black permanent marker

What to Do
1. Cut out the hand and letter patterns. Trace the letters on gold felt and cut them out.
2. Trace the hand on colored felt and cut out one for each child.
3. Fold down the top of the purple felt 1". Place a 35" length of gold ribbon under the fold, centering the ribbon. Fold down the felt 1" a second time. Glue down the fold and tie the ends of the ribbon in a bow.
4. Give each child a hand to glue on the banner. Print the child's name on his or her hand.

Continued on next page...

Praising

55

craft

Continued from previous page...

5. As each child glues a hand on the banner, encourage him or her to say, "I worship God with praise."

6. Hang the banner on the wall outside your classroom for all to enjoy.

Praising

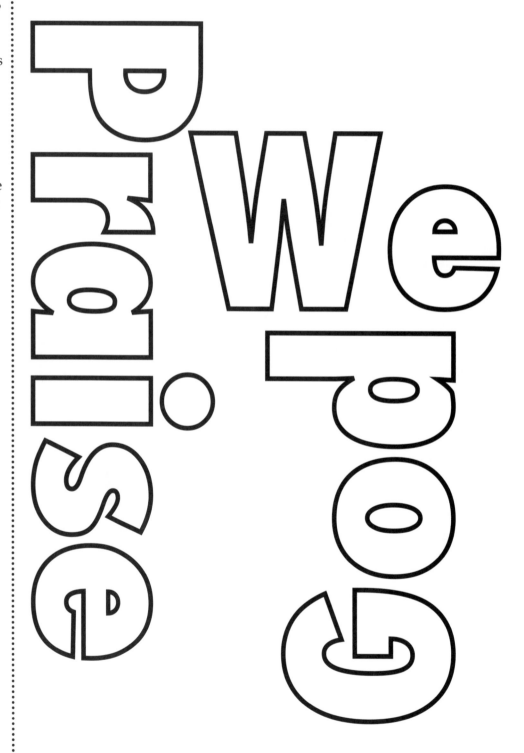

Chapter 6

I Have Fun Praying at Church

 Memory Verse

Pray for each other.
James 5:16

 ## Story to Share

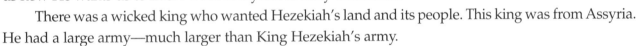 ### Hezekiah Prays in the Temple

King Hezekiah was a wise king who obeyed God's laws. He loved God. He wanted the people of his land to serve God only.

"I want all the altars of false gods destroyed," he said. After the altars were destroyed, he told the people, "God gave us the Ten Commandments to show us how He wants us to live. I want everyone to obey these laws."

There was a wicked king who wanted Hezekiah's land and its people. This king was from Assyria. He had a large army—much larger than King Hezekiah's army.

Hezekiah sent a letter to the Assyrian king, Sennacherib. "Please send your army away," he said. "If you agree to leave my land, I will pay you any price."

King Sennacherib laughed to himself. He demanded that King Hezekiah send him large amounts of silver and gold. When the wicked king received the silver and gold he ordered his soldiers to attack Jerusalem anyway.

"Tell King Hezekiah he must surrender," he instructed his soldiers.

Hezekiah was sad, but he knew God would help him. So he went to the temple to worship God.

"I worship You," he prayed to God. "You made heaven and earth. The angels live in heaven and worship You."

After worshipping, King Hezekiah asked God to help the people of Jerusalem.

Then a prophet, Isaiah, told Hezekiah, "Don't be afraid. God sees how you worship Him in His house. God will defend you and save the city."

That night, God's angel of death flew over the Assyrian camp, killing thousands of the soldiers. When Sennacherib walked out of his tent the next morning, he saw only rows and rows of bodies instead of soldiers ready to fight. Hezekiah's kingdom was safe!

— Based on 2 Kings 19

 ## Discussion Questions

1. Where did King Hezekiah go when he was afraid? (to the temple)
2. What can we do when we are afraid? (Worship God and pray for help)

puzzle

What You Need
- duplicated page
- crayons
- safety scissors
- glue

What to Do
1. Duplicate a worksheet for each child.
2. Allow the children to color and cut out the squares.
3. Instruct them to match each covering to what it covers.

What to Say
Just like the lid covers the pan to protect the food, and the blanket covers the child to protect him from the cold, the prayers we pray are our coverings to protect us from harm.

The Covering of Prayer

Praying

Play and Eat

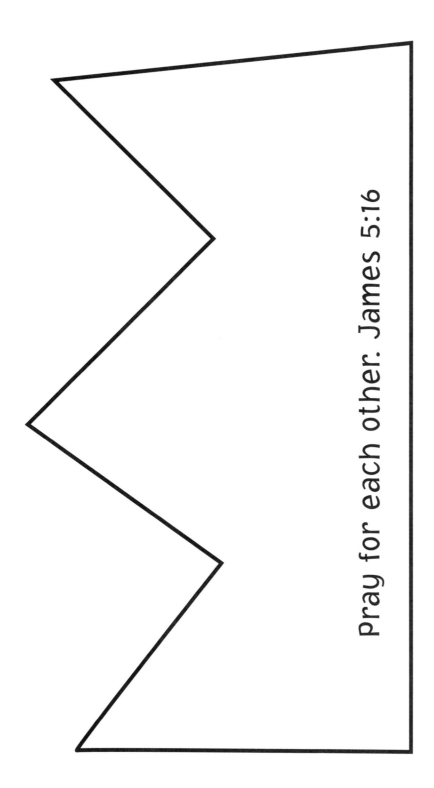

Pray for each other. James 5:16

snack

What You Need
- duplicated page
- wax paper
- squirt cheese
- colored marshmallows
- crackers

What to Do
1. Duplicate a crown pattern for each child.
2. Give each child a pattern and sheet of wax paper. Instruct the children to place the wax paper on top of the crown.
3. Allow the children to use the squirt cheese to follow the outlines of the crowns under their wax paper.
4. Give the children marshmallows to use as gems for the points of their crowns.
5. Allow the children to dip their crackers in the cheese.

Praying

A Real King's Crown

craft

What You Need
• duplicated page
• newspaper
• gold spray paint
• acrylic rhinestones
• glue
• pencil
• tape

What to Do
1. Duplicate a set of words for each child.
2. Spray paint both sides of the newspaper gold.
3. Cut the newspaper lengthwise in 6" widths. Cut 2½" slits across the newspaper every 3 inches (making a fringe). Give each child a strip.
4. Give the children pencils on which to roll the fringed paper for curling.
3. Allow the children to glue the words around their crowns and decorate them with acrylic rhinestones.
4. Adjust each child's crown to fit his or her head. Cut off excess.

Praying

A

Real

King

Worships

God.

Hezekiah's Song

King Hezekiah
worshiped God.
He knew the true God
could answer prayer.
When the enemy tried to
trick him so,
He just let God
take care of his foe.

ribbon

Continued on next page...

song
What You Need
• duplicated page
• construction paper
• crayons
• ribbon
• glue

What to Do
1. Duplicate a temple and king for each child. Cut a 8" length of ribbon for each child.
2. Let the children color the pictures.
3. Assist each child in folding the king piece on the dashed lines, sandwiching one end of the ribbon inside, and gluing the sides together. Help each child sandwich the other end of the ribbon at the top middle of the throne picture and glue the sides together.
4. Show the children how to move the king from his throne to the temple to worship God.
5. Sing the song to the tune of "I'm a Little Teapot" while the children bring King Hezekiah to the temple to pray.

Praying

61

ribbon

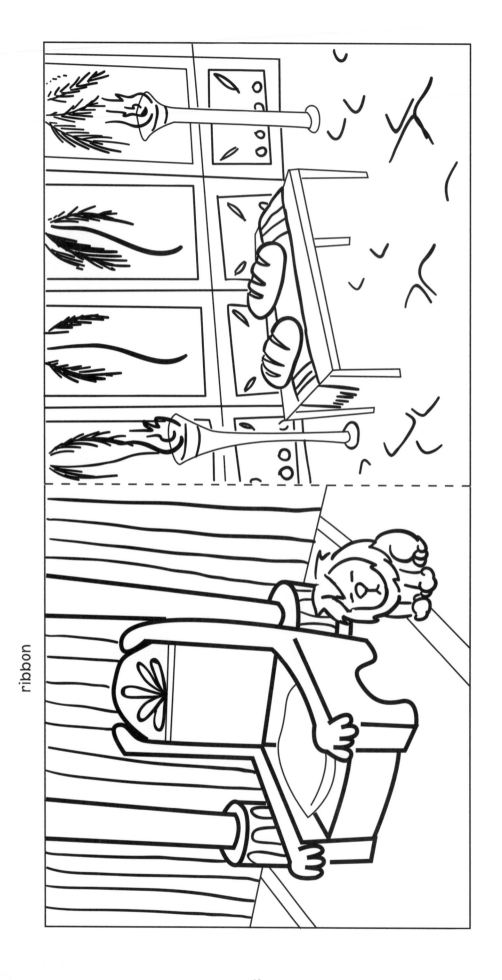

Circle the Answer

King Hezekiah was a wise king who obeyed God's laws.		
King Hezekiah built altars for all the false gods.		
King Sennacherib wanted to take over King Hezekiah's land.		
King Hezekiah said King Sennacherib could have all his video games if he would leave him alone.		
King Sennacherib took silver and gold from King Hezekiah, but he still planned to fight against him.		
King Hezekiah went to the temple to worship and pray to God.		
The prophet Isaiah told the king to go eat an ice cream sundae and everything would be okay.		
God's angel of death killed thousands of the soldiers who fought in King Sennacherib's army.		

puzzle

What You Need
- duplicated page
- crayons

What to Do
1. Duplicate a worksheet for each child.
2. Read each sentence to the children. Instruct them to circle the smiling girl for a "yes" answer, or the frowning girl for a "no" answer.

Answer Key
1. Yes, true.
2. No, false.
3. Yes, true.
4. No, false.
5. Yes, true.
6. Yes, true.
7. No, false.
8. Yes, true.

Praying

puzzle

What You Need
• duplicated page
• crayons

What to Do
1. Duplicate a worksheet for each child.
2. Give each child a yellow crayon to color all the areas with a star.
3. Give each child a green crayon to color all the areas with a cross.
4. Give each child a crayon to match his or her skin color to color all the areas with a smiley face.

What to Say
Hezekiah prayed for God to deliver him. What did Hezekiah do before asking God to help the people of Jerusalem? (He worshipped God.)

Mystery Prayer

Pray for each other. James 5:16

Praying

64

Prayer Reminder Clipboard

Pray for each other.
James 5:16

pray for	pray for
_____	_____

What To Say

Prayer is not limited to worship time in church. You can pray for your family and friends every day.

What You Need
- duplicated page
- card stock
- miniature spring-type clothespins
- crayons
- craft foam sheets
- magnets
- glue

What to Do
1. Duplicate the patterns on card stock and cut out one set for each child.
2. Cut a 2½" x 5" strip of craft foam for each child.
3. Instruct each child to glue the verse to the center of the foam strip, the boy and girl to the clothespins, and the clothespins to the foam strip on either side of the verse.
4. Give each child the two prayer cards to clip to the reminder.
5. Allow the children to glue the magnets to the backs of their reminders.

Praying

Handy Prayers

craft

What You Need
• duplicated page
• yarn
• craft sticks
• glue

What to Do
1. Duplicate and cut out a hand for each child.
2. Give each child a hand and instructions to fold and glue three fingers down, leaving the pointer finger free.
3. Help the children tie bows around their pointer fingers. Explain that some people tie a bow around a finger to help them remember the things they need to do.
4. Print each child's name on his or her hand, along with a prayer request from the child.
5. Allow the children to glue their hands to craft sticks.
6. Put the hands in a sack and allow each child to pick

Continued at right...

Praying

Pray for each other.
James 5:16

Continued from left...

one out (make sure they do not receive their own hands). Read the requests to the child. Have a prayer time, encouraging each child to take a turn at praying for the requests on the hands they picked.

7. The children may take home their chosen hands to remind them to pray for their friends.

What to Say
First, let's thank God for (Emily) and then we'll ask God to help (her grandma feel better).

Chapter 7
I Have Fun Singing at Church

📖 Memory Verse

Sing and make music in your heart to the Lord.
Ephesians 5:19

📖 Story to Share
Singing in the Temple

One of the most wicked kings of Judah was Ahaz. Instead of worshipping the true God, he worshipped a false god named Moloch. Moloch was not a true, living God. He could not see, could not hear and could not love those who worshipped him.

King Ahaz set up false gods in every city of Judah. Then he turned God's temple into a place to worship these false gods. He forced the priests to worship them, too.

King Ahaz was only 36 years old when he died, but he left his evil influence over Judah. When he died, his son, Hezekiah, became king.

King Hezekiah did not follow his father's ways. He served the true God. He ordered the priests to clean and repair the temple so it could be used to worship God. After all the idols were removed, and the furnishings were fixed, Hezekiah ordered a special service to rededicate the temple to God's work.

What a time of worship the people had in the temple! There were many instruments, such as cymbals, harps and trumpets, playing praise music to God. There were singers who sang their praises to God. They sang the songs that King David had written — some while he had been a shepherd looking after his father's sheep. Joy was bubbling in their hearts as they sang their praises. Those who heard the singers bowed their heads and worshipped with them. King Hezekiah rejoiced with them, happy to see the temple being used in worship to the true God.

— Based on 2 Chronicles 29

❓ Discussion Questions

1. What are some ways the people in the temple worshipped God? (by playing instruments and singing)
2. Can you worship God in this way?

Heart Music

What You Need
- duplicated patterns
- red craft foam
- red construction paper
- music scores/sheet music
- black permanent marker
- lettering
- stapler
- crayons
- paper bag

What to Do
1. Duplicate a face for each child. Cut off ponytails for boy faces.
2. Using the heart pattern, cut one heart from red foam and one from red construction paper for each child.
3. Duplicate the music scores and attach them to the bulletin board as a border.
4. Give each child a face to color.
5. Ask each child what his or her favorite song is and print the title

Continued on next page...

Singing

68

Continued from left...

on the foam and construction paper hearts with the child's name printed in smaller letters underneath the title.

6. Attach lettering to the board that says "We're Making Music to the Lord in Our Hearts."

7. Staple each child's paper head to the foam heart and attach the figures randomly on the board.

8. Place the construction paper hearts in a bag. Periodically throughout the class time, have a child reach in and draw a heart. Sing the song on the heart.

Sing and make music in your heart to the Lord. Ephesians 5:19

Singing

puzzle

What You Need
- duplicated page
- crayons

What to Do
1. Duplicate a worksheet for each child.
2. Instruct the children to find the items from the boxed area in their pictures, and circle the items.
3. Allow the children to color their pictures.

What to Say
Let's count how many people are singing and worshipping God. See the smiles on their faces? Worshipping God is a happy thing to do.

Can You Find It?

Singing

Bottled Music

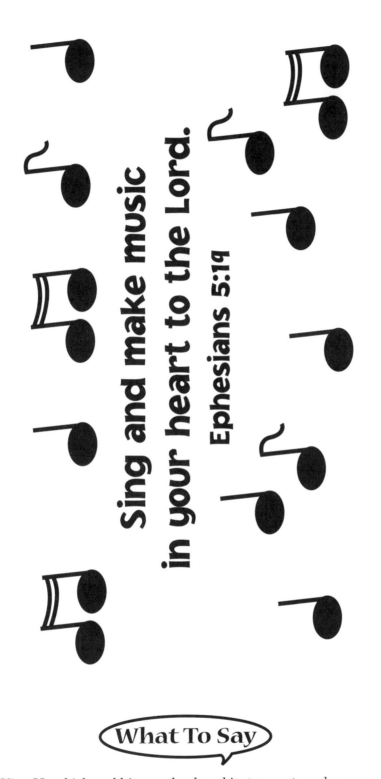

Sing and make music in your heart to the Lord.
Ephesians 5:19

What To Say

Just like King Hezekiah and his people played instruments and sang praises to God as they worshipped in the temple, we can sing a praise chorus to Him, too.

craft

What You Need

- bottle wrap
- chenille stems
- plastic soft-drink bottles
- black buttons
- glue
- rice, beans, pebbles, macaroni for filler
- funnel

What to Do

1. Duplicate a bottle wrap for each child.
2. Give each child a bottle and allow the child to choose a filler. Pour about ⅛ cup of filler into the bottle.
3. Allow the children to glue black buttons to the circles for notes.
4. Help the children glue the wraps around the bottles.
5. Spread glue inside each cap and twist it on tightly.
6. Tie two chenille stems around each bottle's neck. Show how to curl the ends on a pencil.
7. Sing a praise chorus as the children shake their instruments.

Singing

A Bubbling Heart

snack

What You Need
- duplicated page
- apples
- cinnamon
- sugar
- plastic sandwich bags
- crayons
- cups
- straws
- juice and club soda
- hole punch

What to Do
1. Duplicate and cut out a heart for each child. Punch holes where indicated. Slice apples. Mix cinnamon and sugar. Place one teaspoon of the mixture in a plastic sandwich bag for each child.
2. Let the children color their hearts.
3. Show how to slide the heart onto a straw.
4. Give each child a plastic sandwich bag and four apple slices. Tell the children to shake their bags as you sing the song to the tune of "The Farmer in the Dell."

I sing and worship God.
I sing and worship God.
His love is in my heart,
Bubbling from the start.

Sing and make music in your heart to the Lord.

Ephesians 5:19

Singing

72

Kingly Verse Review

Sing and make music in your heart to the Lord.

-Ephesians 5:19

game

What You Need
- duplicated page
- card stock
- crayons
- gems
- elastic
- stapler
- clear tape

What to Do
1. Duplicate a crown to card stock, decorate it and cut it out.
2. Cut a piece of elastic the length of the crown and staple each elastic end to a crown side. Cover the staples with tape to prevent injury.
3. Tell the children to sit in a circle. Choose one child to be king. The king walks around the circle and chooses a child on whom to put the crown. The child wearing the crown then stands up, joins hands with the king and skips around the circle singing the memory verse to a made-up tune. The old king then sits in the empty spot.

Singing

craft

What You Need
- duplicated page
- crayons
- gold glitter glue

What to Do
1. Duplicate and cut out the kings and throne for each child.
2. Allow the children to color their kings and thrones.
3. Tell the children to squeeze the glitter glue on the crowns.
4. Read the statements below and let the children to put the correct king on the throne.

Two Kings Play Set

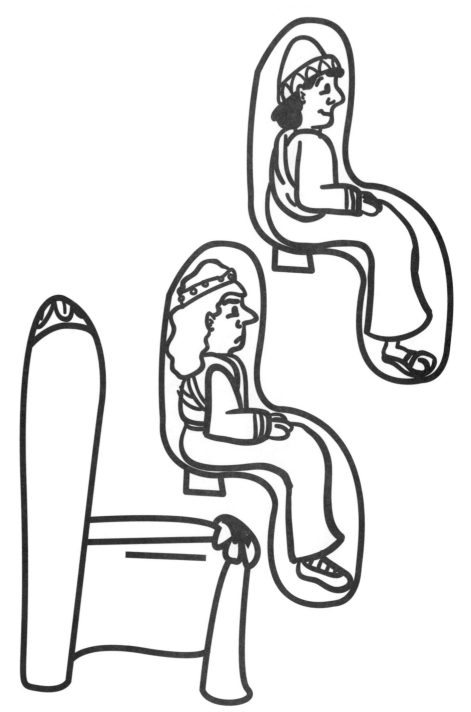

This king was one of the wickedest kings in Judah. (Ahaz)
This king became king after Ahaz died. (Hezekiah)
This king worshiped Moloch, not the true, living God. (Ahaz)
This king served the true God. (Hezekiah)
This king set up false gods in every city in Judah. (Ahaz)
This king removed all the false gods from the temple and from Judah. (Hezekiah)
This king forced the priests to worship the false gods. (Ahaz)
This king sang with the worshippers of God in the temple. (Hezekiah)

Singing

A Story in Questions

activity

What You Need
• duplicated page
• crayons

What to Do
1. Duplicate a worksheet for each child.
2. Instruct the children to look at the first box. Read the first question and allow the children to discuss the answer together.
3. Instruct the children to color the picture and correct answer, and draw a large "X" on the wrong answer.

Who did the bad King Ahaz worship? (Moloch)
What did Hezekiah become when his father died? (king)
What did Hezekiah have repaired? (the temple)
What did the people do in the temple? (sang praise music to God)

Singing

Rebus Verse

What You Need
- duplicated page
- crayons

What to Do

1. Duplicate and cut out a set of memory verse pictures for yourself and for each child.
2. Before class, color your set of pictures. Use them to teach the memory verse. (Hold up the child singing for "sing," the note for "make music," the heart for "in your heart" and the picture of Jesus for "to the Lord.")
3. Give the children their own sets of verse pictures. Allow the children to color the pictures and then tell the verse to each other, using the pictures.

Singing

Chapter 8
I Have Fun with Others at Church

Memory Verse

Let us exalt His name together.
Psalm 34:3

Story to Share
Gathered Together

One day after Jesus went back to heaven, the disciples were meeting together with other believers. Mary, Jesus' mother, was there with them. There were about 120 people worshipping God.

Peter stood to speak.

"Judas betrayed Jesus," he told the crowd. "Even if he was alive he would not be worthy to be a disciple. We need to decide on someone to take his place."

The other disciples agreed. The people prayed that they would choose the right man for this important job. They knew only God could see their hearts. With His leading, the disciples chose Matthias as the next disciple.

Later, when it was time for Pentecost, a Jewish harvest festival, the disciples gathered together again. This time while they were worshipping, they heard a sound like a loud wind. It wasn't the wind blowing from the outside — the sound was in the room! Suddenly, as they looked at each other they saw tiny flames hovering over each of their heads. The Holy Spirit had come to bless them and their time together.

People from many different countries had come for the festival. They saw that God was with the disciples, too. Many people believed in Christ that day — nearly 3,000! Peter baptized the people who wanted to follow Christ.

— Based on Acts 2

Discussion Questions

1. Did the disciples have a church in which to worship? (no)
2. Does the place we worship matter to God? (no, He just wants us to worship with other believers)

puzzle

What You Need
• duplicated page
• crayons

What to Do
1. Duplicate a worksheet for each child.
2. Discuss the pictures, then give the commands. Use gentle questions to assist those who need help (e.g., "Can you see the glue bottle?").
3. Allow the children to color the pictures.

What to Say
When we gather together to worship, we do many different things: we hear a Bible story, we pray together and we work on crafts. Whatever activity we choose as part of our worship, the Holy Spirit visits us with His joy.

With Others

Activity Recognition Fun

1. Draw a circle around the picture of the children making a craft project.
2. Draw a triangle around the picture of the children singing together.
3. Draw a square around the picture of the children praying together.
4. Draw a rectangle around the picture of the children listening to a Bible story.

Scissors Walks

79

game

What You Need

- duplicated page
- craft foam sheets
- crayons
- zipper-top plastic snack bags
- permanent marker

What to Do

1. Duplicate and cut out a set of game discs for each child.
2. Cut foam sheets into 6" squares. Using a permanent marker, make a tic-tac-toe grid, with 1½" squares, for each child.
3. Allow the children to color their sets of game discs. Provide resealable plastic snack bags for their discs.
4. Have the children choose partners. Ask the review questions. Allow group answers — then the children may each have a turn on their tic-tac-toe boards.

With Others

Tic-Tac-Toe Review

Is God happy when we worship together? (yes)

Say the memory verse to tell God's command for worship. (Let us exalt His name together.)

Did Peter and the disciples obey this command? (yes)

Who was chosen to replace Judas as a disciple? (Matthias)

Which harvest festival were the people celebrating in Jerusalem? (Pentecost)

What did they hear while the disciples were gathered together? (A sound like the wind)

What did they see above their heads? (tiny flames)

Who had come to bless them and their time together? (the Holy Spirit)

Who will come and bless our time together? (the Holy Spirit)

Song for the Band

We worship with our friends,
Just like the Bible says.
Give me your hand, come join our band,
As we worship God! (YEAH!)

Let us exalt His name together. Psalm 34:3

song

What You Need
- duplicated page
- paper towel tubes
- tube wrap pattern
- crayons
- stickers
- glue
- chenille stems
- jingle bells
- hole punch

What to Do
1. Cut the paper towel tubes in half. You will need one half for each child. Cut chenille stems in thirds, three for each child.
2. Duplicate a tube wrap for each child.
3. Allow the children to print their names on the wraps.
4. Assist the children in gluing their wraps to the tubes.
5. Allow the children to decorate the wraps with stickers.
6. Punch three holes, an equal distance apart, on one end of each wrapped tube.
7. Give each child three jingle bells

Continued at left...

Continued from right...

and three chenille stem pieces. Show how to slide the jingle bell on a chenille stem, put one end of the stem through the hole and twist the ends together.

8. Choose a child to be the song leader. March with the leader around the room, singing the song to the tune of "The B-I-B-L-E," as the leader shakes his or her instrument. At the end of the song, the leader should touch another child on the hand and that child can join the group to sing the song and march. Continue until all the children have been chosen.

With Others

What You Need
- duplicated page
- fluorescent poster board
- scissors
- crayons

What to Do
1. Duplicate and cut out enough word strips to complete the project.
2. Have each child trace around his or her foot and cut out the shape.
3. Instruct the children to make faces out of their cut-out feet.
4. Attach the feet to the wall for a border. In between each foot place a word strip.

What to Say
Our feet look happy they came to worship. Do you have a smile on your face, too?

With Others

Foot Portrait Wall Border

Let	us
exalt	His
name	together.

Handy Friendship Wreath

craft

What You Need
- duplicated page
- glue
- ribbon
- poster board
- yarn
- ribbon bow
- tape

What to Do
1. Duplicate and cut out a verse circle and six hands for each child.
2. Cut a 6" circle from poster board for each child.
3. Instruct the children to glue their verse circles to the centers of the poster boards.
4. Show how to glue the hands on the edges of the poster boards, overlapping to fit.
5. Allow the children to print their names on their friends' hands.
6. Give each child a pre-tied bow to glue to the top of the wreath.
7. Tape a yarn hoop to the back of the wreath for hanging.

Let us exalt His name together.

Psalm 34:3

With Others

snack

What You Need

- duplicated page
- colored paper
- hole punch
- curling ribbon
- zipper-top plastic sandwich bags
- fruit-flavored puffed cereal
- fruit-flavored cereal circles
- fruit-flavored gummy candy

What to Do

1. Duplicate a verse card to colored paper and cut out one for each child.
2. Mix the cereal and candy together. Allow each child to dip a cup in the mixture and pour some in a bag. Seal the bags afterward.
3. Assist each child in punching a hole in the corner of the verse card and in the plastic bag. Thread a length of ribbon through, tie and curl the ends.
4. Make sure you have extra fruity mixture for snacking!

With Others

Differently the Same

Look at the mixture we made. It all tastes like fruit, but some of the cereal looks like round balls and some of the cereal looks like tiny doughnuts. The candy looks different from the cereal. Look around at your friends. You're all kids, but you're different. (Abigail) has blue eyes and (Daniel) has brown eyes. (Olivia) has blond hair and (Jacob) has black hair. (Zachary) is tall and (Hannah) is short. God loves us just the way we are, and He loves to see all the different ways we worship together.

Lift the Flap Story Picture

craft

What You Need

- duplicated page
- construction paper
- glue
- crayons

What to Do

1. Duplicate a story picture for each child.
2. Cut construction paper sheets in half. Cut a three-sided door in a construction paper half for each child. Print "Jesus is with us" on the door.
3. Give each child a picture to color. Instruct the children to glue the pictures to the uncut half sheets of construction paper.
4. Assist the children in gluing the cut papers to the pictures along the edges. Show the children how to open the doors to see the pictures.

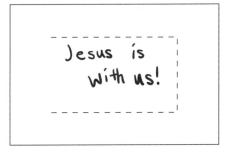

Jesus was with the disciples when they worshipped together. Jesus is with us, today, while we worship together, too. We can feel His presence in our hearts.

With Others

Chapter 9
Miscellaneous

Teacher Welcome

What You Need
- duplicated page and page 87
- bright paper
- yarn
- clear, self-stick plastic

What to Do

1. Duplicate the teacher on page 87 (enlarging if possible). Color the picture, cover it with clear plastic and cut it out.

2. Duplicate a student tag to bright paper for each child. Print each child's name on a tag. Cover with clear plastic and cut out.

3. Punch holes where indicated. Tie 24" lengths of yarn through the holes to make necklace tags.

4. Attach the teacher to your door, leaving the teacher's hands free. Add the words, "(Mrs. Kuhn) Welcomes You" to the door.

Continued at right...

Miscellaneous

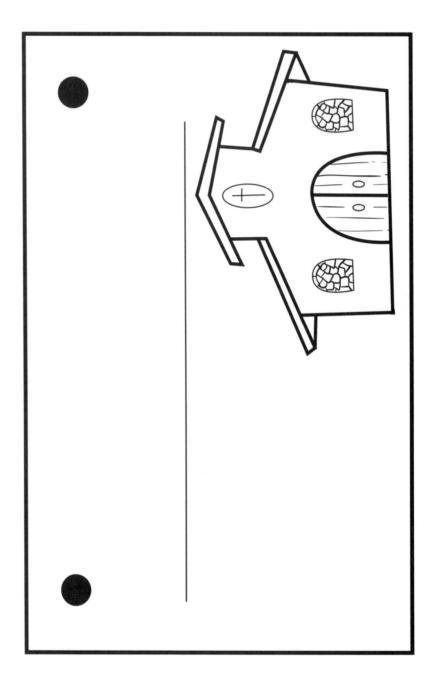

Continued from left...

5. As the children enter your room, allow them to find their tags and wear them for the class time.

6. When everyone has arrived, lay the extra tags aside. These will remind you to send "missing you" notes to the absentees. Make a few blank tags for visitors or new students.

Worship Body Play

I may be just a little kid
(stoop down)
Short, not very tall.
(stand, reaching for the sky)
But I can worship lots of ways;
(hands on hips, nodding head)
And give God my all.
(hands outstretched)

God loves to feel our hugs,
(hug self)
"I love you" is what we say.
(sign language for I love you)
I can wave my hands in joy,
(wave hands)
Or bow my head to pray.
(bow head, fold hands)

What You Need
• duplicated page

What to Do
1. Show the children how to perform the actions.
2. Read each line and have the children perform the action that goes along with the line.
3. Repeat the whole Worship Body Play, encouraging the children to say the words and perform the actions with you.

What to Say
Even a child can worship God. Try each day to tell God you love Him.

Miscellaneous

89

A Hug for God

craft

What You Need
- duplicated page
- colored card stock
- small stickers
- flesh-colored crayons
- translucent thread
- glue

What to Do
1. Duplicate and cut out a set of hands for each child. Cut card stock into 3" x 11" strips.
2. Assist the children with printing their names on the lines.
3. Allow the children to color the hands the shades of their skin.
4. Give each child a paper strip to make arms. Allow the children to decorate their arms with stickers and crayons. Assist the children with rolling the strips, then unrolling to make a slight curl.
5. Instruct the children to glue the hands on the ends of the arms.
6. Hang the hugs

Continued at right...

Miscellaneous

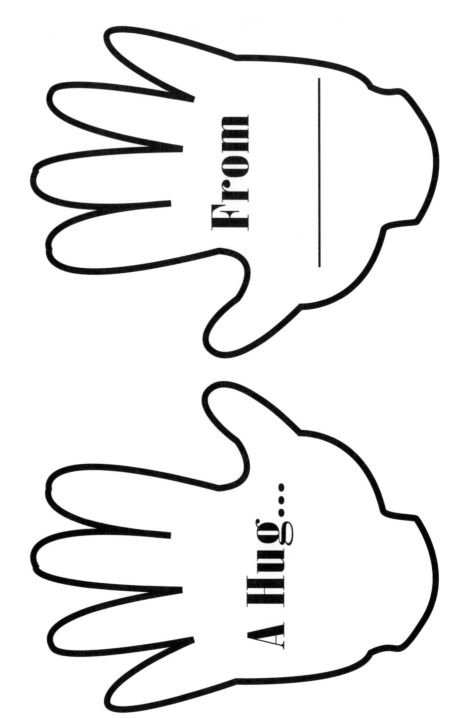

From

A Hug...

Continued from left...
from the ceiling around the room, using translucent threads cut at various lengths.

What to Say
One way we know someone loves us is when he or she gives us a big hug. Worshipping God is like giving Him a big hug. When we worship God, we're telling Him we love Him and we're happy to belong to Him.

Absentee Postcard

What You Need
- duplicated page
- card stock
- crayons

What to Do
1. Duplicate the postcard to cardstock.
2. Lay out the postcards and crayons for early arrivals to color.
3. Later, draw a line through the middle of the back of each postcard. Address the right side and attach a stamp. Write a short personal note on the left side.
4. Mention the children who are absent that day. Pray a simple prayer for each absent child by name. (Mail the postcards immediately so they won't be mislaid or forgotten!)

Miscellaneous

Certificate of Worship

craft

What You Need
• duplicated page
• crayons
• glue

What to Do
1. Duplicate and cut out a certificate and church for each child.
2. Allow the children to color the churches.
3. Show the children where to glue the churches.
4. Print each child's name and the date where indicated and sign your name.

Certificate of Worship

Has earned a Worship Certificate for Faithful Worship.

Teacher

Date

Church Is Fun Book

activity

What You Need
• duplicated page
• crayons

What to Do
1. Duplicate and cut out (around the outer edge) a book for each student.
2. Allow the children to color their books.
3. Instruct the children to fold the books in half lengthwise, then accordion-style, and to press the edges together firmly.
4. Encourage the children to share the story with classmates.

Miscellaneous

teacher help

What You Need
• duplicated page
• stickers

What to Do
1. Duplicate a parent letter for each family in your church. (Many times those who do not have children are happy to help with gathering materials.)
2. Fold each letter in thirds and seal the flap with a sticker.

Miscellaneous

Will You Help?

Will You Help?

Dear Parents and Friends of our Preschoolers,

We're planning on having a blast worshipping God while we use the unit theme "I Have Fun at Church!" If you have any of these items we need for our classroom experience, please share them with us.

• black and brown felt
• red foam sheets
• Bingo daubers
• paper plates: dinner and dessert size
• clear self-stick plastic
• miniature spring-type clothespins
• plastic drinking straws
• masking tape
• chenille stems
• gold glitter glue
• elastic
• plastic gems
• resealable sandwich bags
• craft sticks
• magnetic tape
• cotton balls
• gold spray paint
• paper fasteners

Thank you!

_____
teacher

Progressive Bulletin Board

bulletin board

What You Need
- duplicated pages
- digital camera
- lettering

What to Do
1. Enlarge and cut out the church on page 96. Color it, and attach it to the middle of the board.
2. Attach lettering for "Church is Fun!" to the board.
3. Duplicate, cut out and color the theme symbols. Add a theme symbol at each class session to introduce the lesson.
4. Take a picture of the children acting out the lesson themes. Develop the pictures and use them to review each Sunday, attaching the pictures to the board beside the coordinating symbol.

Continued on next page...

Miscellaneous

worship
giving
inviting others
learning
praise
praying
singing
with others

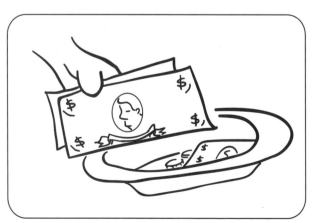